1 2 3

three

Numbers can be written as both words and numerals. You'll see both in this book.

Try to trace this number.

One stroke

Most numbers can be written with one stroke of a pen. Start at the dot (number 1) and follow the arrows.

Try to trace this number.

Two strokes

This number is written with two strokes. Start at the dot (number 1) and follow the arrows. Then put the pen at number 2 and follow the arrows.

Try to trace this number.

Numbers are made up of lots of shapes.

Circles.

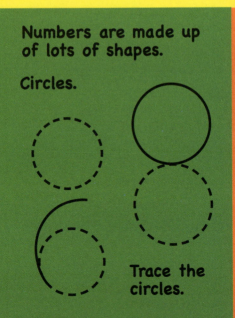

Trace the circles.

Straight lines.

Trace the lines.

Diagonals.

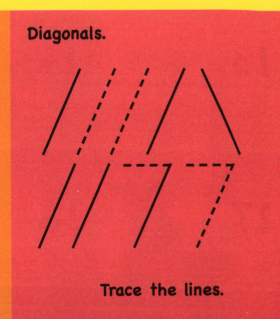

Trace the lines.

Correct order.

Dot-to-dots are a good way to learn the correct order of numbers.

Look carefully to follow the numbers in order.

Join the dots around the cow.

Make a habit of counting.

Count as often as you can. The more you do, the better you will get.

How many flowers can you count here? Write the number in the box.

Counting out groups.

It helps to say numbers aloud as you count.

Count any group of 4 apples. Circle the group.

Look for items to count.

There are items to count all around us, such as buttons and stripes on our clothes.

Tracing numbers.

The more often you trace the numbers in this book, the better you will get.

Try to trace this number.

Count the buttons and then trace the circles.

1
one

Here is 1 ball.
Trace the ball.

How many toys are in the dog's bed? ▢

Here is 1 bowl.
Trace the bowl.

Draw a circle around 1 dog biscuit.

How many brown spots has the puppy got? ▢

Circle 1 biscuit.

Write 1 inside the shape.

Write 1 by joining up the dashes.

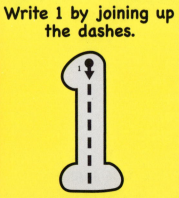

Write 1 between the lines.

_____

How many people are on the bus?

2

two

How many girls can you count?

Draw a circle around 2 red flowers.

Trace 2 wheels on the car.

Write 2 on the car.

Circle 2 wheels.

Write 2 inside the shape.

Write 2 by joining up the dashes.

Write 2 between the lines.

3

three

How many spoons can you see?

How many forks can you see?

How many knives can you see?

Trace 3 eggs.

Trace 3 plates.

Trace 3 apples in the bowl.

Draw 3 more apples.

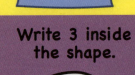

Write 3 on the cup.

Circle 3 peas.

Write 3 inside the shape.

Write 3 by joining up the dashes.

Write 3 between the lines.

_____

_____

Trace the number 4 on the party hat.

Draw 4 candles on the cake.

4
four

Draw 4 strawberries on the cake.

Draw 4 straws in the cups.

Count the parcels and write the number in the box.

Circle 4 cherries.

Write 4 inside the shape.

Write 4 by joining up the dashes.

Write 4 between the lines.

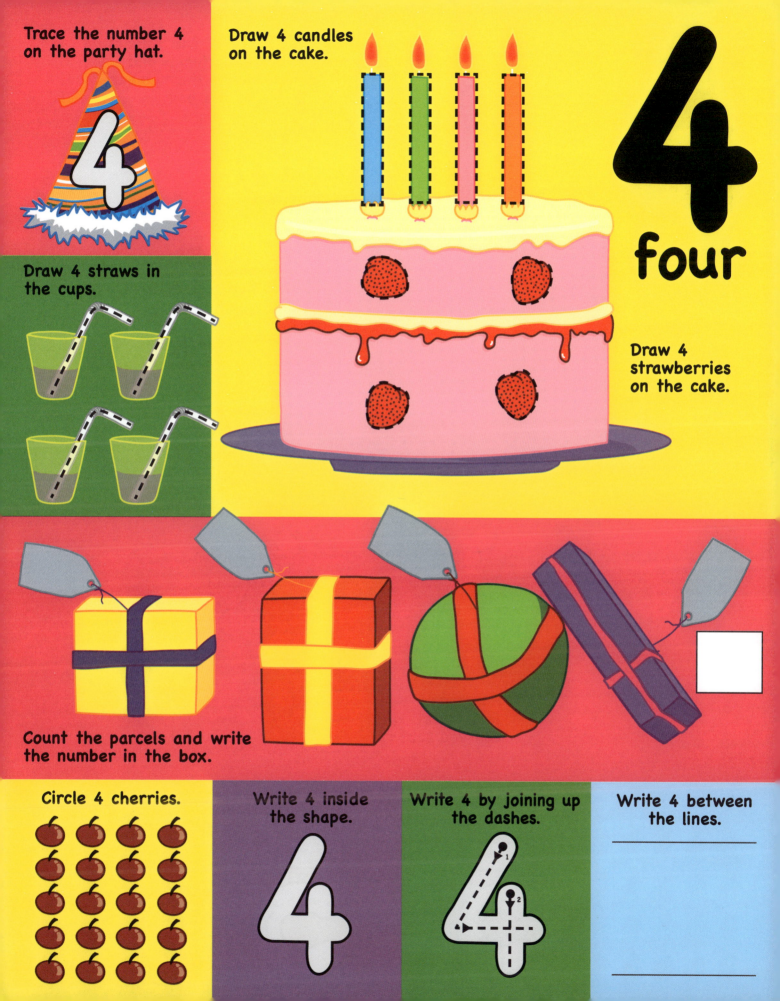

5
five

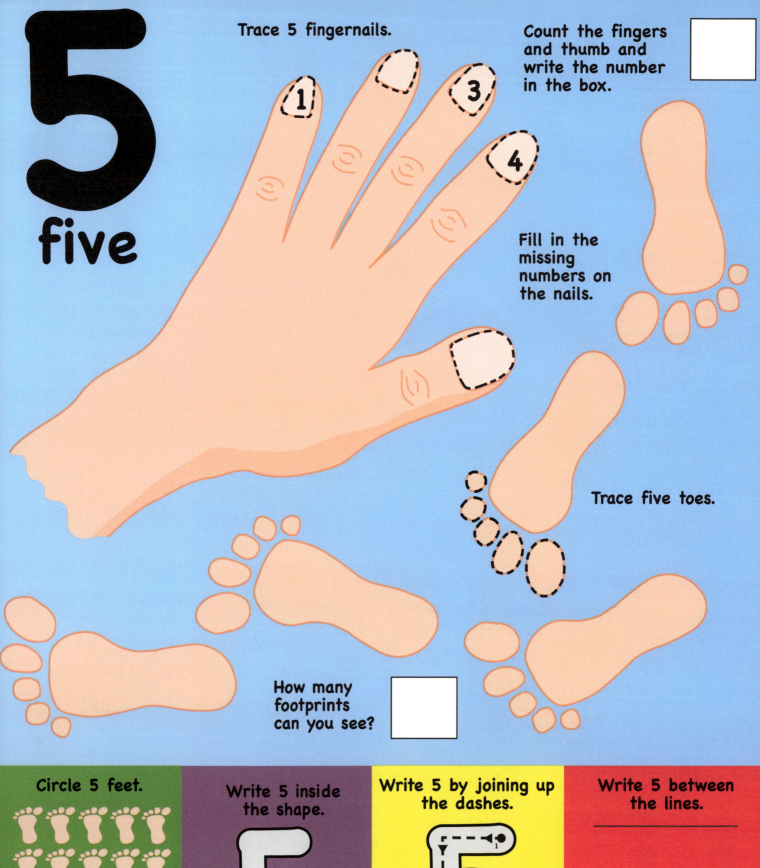

Trace 5 fingernails.

Count the fingers and thumb and write the number in the box.

Fill in the missing numbers on the nails.

Trace five toes.

How many footprints can you see?

Circle 5 feet.

Write 5 inside the shape.

Write 5 by joining up the dashes.

Write 5 between the lines.

Count the yellow stripes on the caterpillar and write the number in the box.

Fill in the missing numbers on the beetles.

6
six

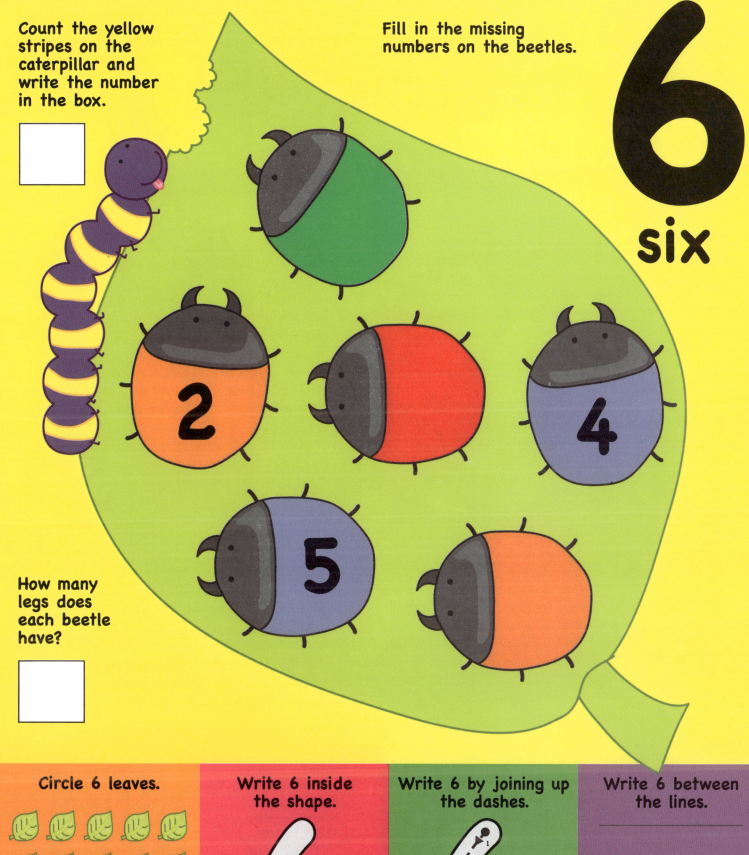

How many legs does each beetle have?

Circle 6 leaves.

Write 6 inside the shape.

Write 6 by joining up the dashes.

Write 6 between the lines.

7
seven

Count the steam puffs and write the number in the box.

Trace the number 7 in the smoke puff.

There are seven people on the train. Trace two of the passengers.

Fill in the missing numbers on the carriages.

Circle 7 wheels.

Write 7 inside the shape.

7

Write 7 by joining up the dashes.

Write 7 between the lines.

How many knights
can you see?

Trace the number 8
on the flag.

8
eight

Trace 3 more
windows.
How many
are there
all together?

Circle 8 shields.

Write 8 inside
the shape.

8

Write 8 by joining up
the dashes.

8

Write 8 between
the lines.

9
nine

Trace the number 9 on the rocket.

Trace the dotted line to join up the stars in the right order.

1 2 3 4 5 6 7 8 9

How many stars can you see?

Countdown to lift-off!

Trace the numbers 5, 4, 3, 2, 1.

5 4 3 2 1

Circle 9 stars.

Write 9 inside the shape.

9

Write 9 by joining up the dashes.

9

Write 9 between the lines.

Trace the number 10 on the glove.

10

How many raindrops can you count?

[ ]

How many buttons can you count?

[ ]

Trace ten buttons.

10
ten

Fill in the missing numbers on the boots.

1 2 3 5 8 10

Circle 10 raindrops.

Write 10 inside the shape.

10

Write 10 by joining up the dashes.

10

Write 10 between the lines.

_____

_____

11
eleven

Trace the dotted line to join up the apples in the right order.

How many leaves are on the ground? Circle the right number.

10   8   4   11   9   6

How many birds can you count in the tree?

Circle 11 apples.

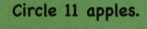

Write 11 inside the shape.

Write 11 by joining up the dashes.

Write 11 between the lines.

_____

_____

Fill in the missing numbers on the cat's footprints.

12

8

4

2

1

How many kittens can you count?

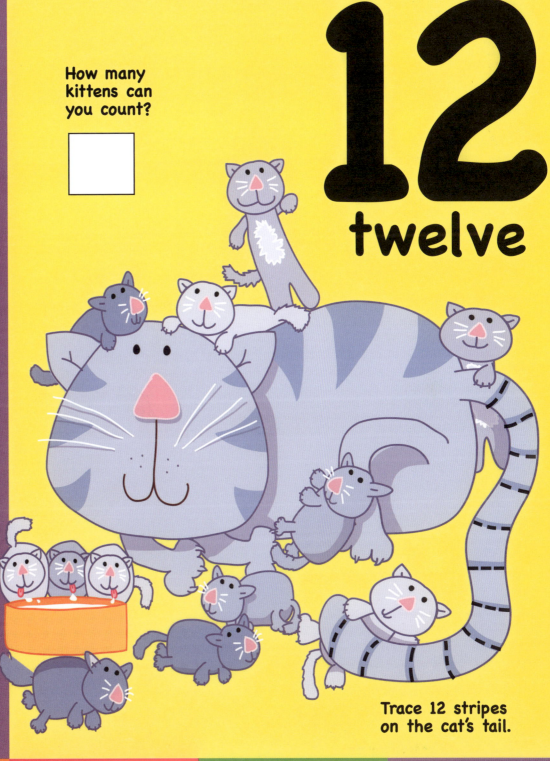

12
twelve

Trace 12 stripes on the cat's tail.

Circle 12 cat biscuits.

Write 12 inside the shape.

12

Write 12 by joining up the dashes.

Write 12 between the lines.

13
thirteen

Trace 4 petals on the flower. How many petals are there altogether?

How many leaves can you count on the flower?

Count the holes at the end of the watering can. Write the number in the box.

Count the butterflies and write the total number on the biggest butterfly.

Circle 13 flowers.

Write 13 inside the shape.

13

Write 13 by joining up the dashes.

Write 13 between the lines.

_____
_____

Count the grapes and circle the correct number below.

9   14   12

Draw 5 more apples.

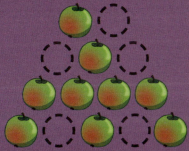

How many apples are there?

14
fourteen

How many cereal flakes are falling into the bowl?

How many blue and white stripes can you count?

Circle 14 cups.

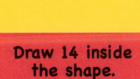

Draw 14 inside the shape.

Write 14 by joining up the dashes.

Write 14 between the lines.

15
fifteen

Join the dots to complete the cow.

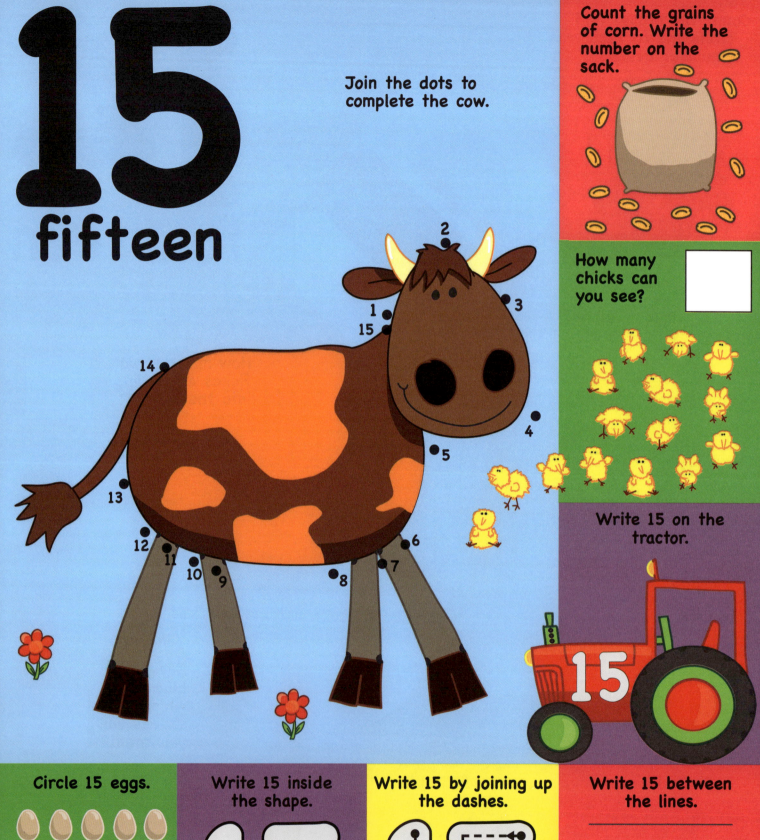

Count the grains of corn. Write the number on the sack.

How many chicks can you see?

Write 15 on the tractor.

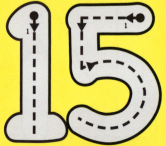

Circle 15 eggs.

Write 15 inside the shape.

Write 15 by joining up the dashes.

Write 15 between the lines.

Write 16 on the cloud.

16

16
sixteen

How many flowers can you see?

Write the missing numbers on the slide.

1
3
4
7
11
14

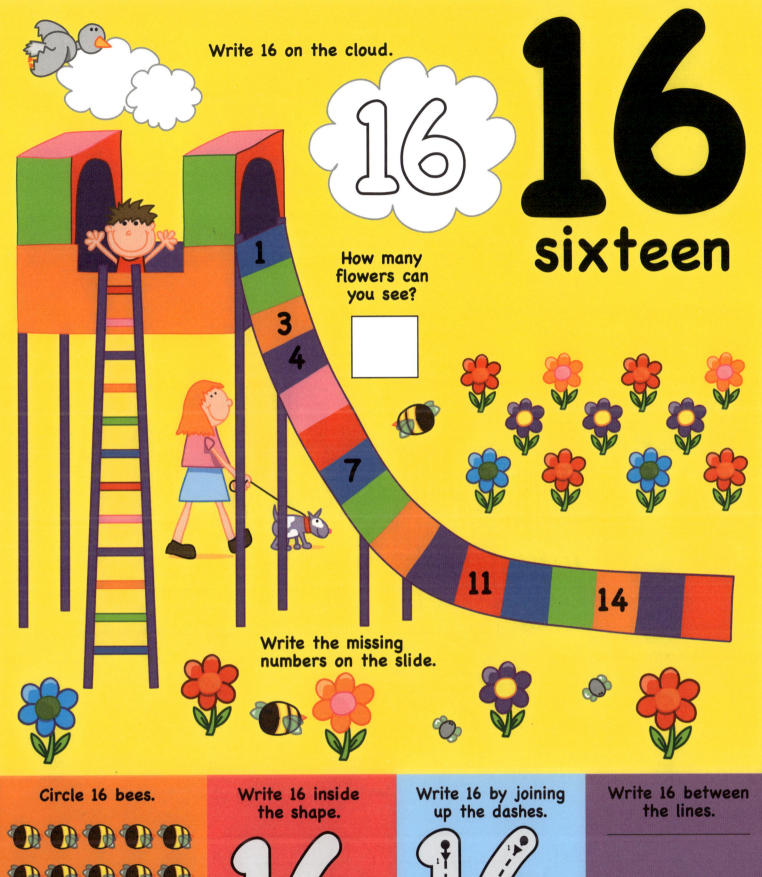

Circle 16 bees.

Write 16 inside the shape.

16

Write 16 by joining up the dashes.

16

Write 16 between the lines.

17
seventeen

How many bananas can you see?

Draw 5 more stripes on the tiger. How many stripes are there on the tiger's body?

How many blue stripes are there on the snake?

Circle 17 leaves.	Write 17 inside the shape.	Write 17 by joining up the dashes.	Write 17 between the lines.

Trace 10 rays on the Sun. How many rays are there?

How many little drops of water can you see spraying from the whale?

Count the feet on the penguins and write the number in the box.

18
eighteen

Count the fish and circle the correct number below.

16   18   9

Circle 18 starfish.

Write 18 inside the shape.

18

Write 18 by joining up the dashes.

Write 18 between the lines.

_____

_____

19
nineteen

Write 19 on the flag.

How many sails can you see?

Trace the dotted line to join up the big spots in the correct order.

Draw 3 more shells to make 19 shells.

Circle 19 jellyfish.

Write 19 inside the shape.

Write 19 by joining up the dashes.

Write 19 between the lines.

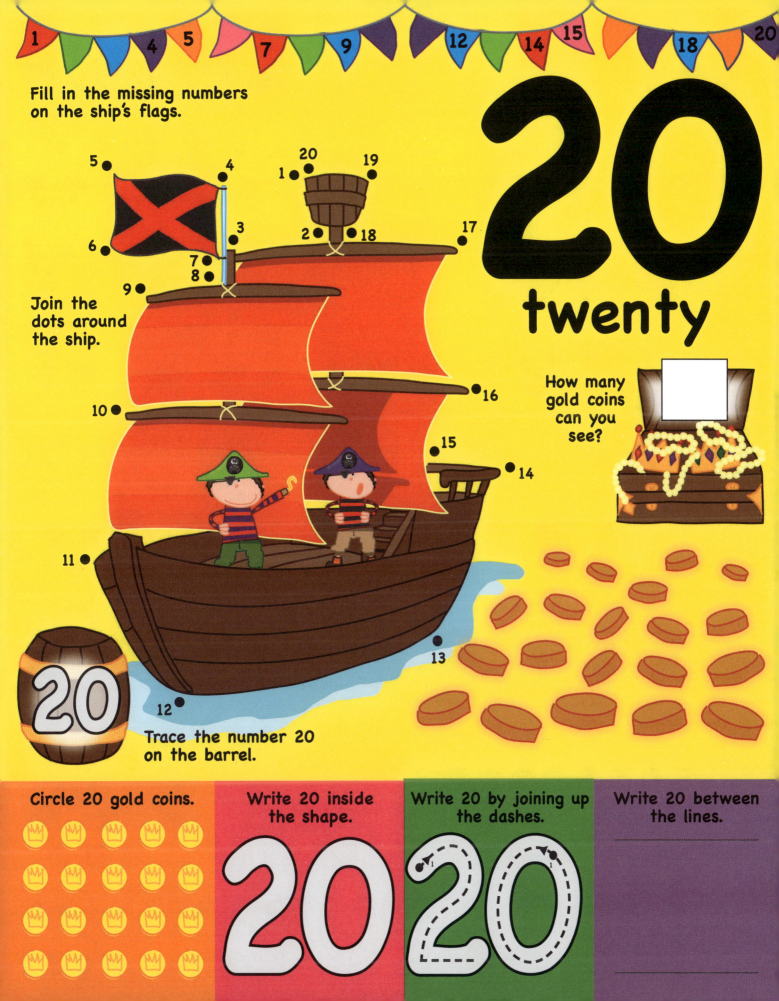

Fill in the missing numbers on the ship's flags.

Join the dots around the ship.

20
twenty

How many gold coins can you see?

Trace the number 20 on the barrel.

Circle 20 gold coins.

Write 20 inside the shape.

Write 20 by joining up the dashes.

Write 20 between the lines.

Count the pictures in each row!

Trace the dotted lines to complete the numbers and pictures.

Write in the missing numbers.